~The~ Thanksgiving Activity Book

by Deborah Schecter

SCHOLASTIC
PROFESSIONAL BOOKS

New York • Toronto • London • Auckland • Sydney
Mexico City • New Delhi • Hong Kong

For Diane, who continues our family's Thanksgiving traditions.

We Give Thanks

For family and friends,
pie and turkey, too
Thanksgiving's the time
we say thank you!

I am thankful for

my family

Name Diane

Acknowledgments

Thanks to Nancy Eldredge, Manager of Education, Wampanoag Indian Program, Plimoth Plantation, Plymouth, Massachusetts, and to Tobias Vanderhoop, Consultant, Wampanoag Tribe of Gay Head Aquinnah, Aquinnah, Massachusetts.

Credits

Quote on page 7 from Plimoth Plantation Almanack (Fall 1998) by the late Nanepashemet, Wampanoag historian and former Director of the Wampanoag Indian Program at Plimoth Plantation, Plymouth, Massachusetts.

"I Can Hardly Wait" and "Funny Turkey" adapted from *Thematic Units for Kindergarten* by Kristen Schlosser (Scholastic Professional Books, 1994). Used by permission of Scholastic Professional Books.

Perky Turkey Puppet adapted from *Peanut Butter* magazine, Number 47. Copyright © 1990 by Scholastic.

"Thanksgiving Day" by Meish Goldish from *Thematic Poems, Songs, and Fingerplays* by Meish Goldish (Scholastic Professional Books, 1993). Used by permission of Scholastic Professional Books.

Cover art by Judith Hoffman Corwin
Cover design by Jaime Lucero
Interior art by Maxie Chambliss, Rusty Fletcher, and James Graham Hale
Interior design by Sydney Wright

ISBN: 0-439-24119-7
Copyright © 2000 by Deborah Schecter
All rights reserved.
Printed in the U.S.A.

Contents

◆ Includes a reproducible activity page

Introduction

Welcome to *The Thanksgiving Activity Book*, a bountiful collection of ready-to-use activities, age-perfect poetry, and hands-on reproducibles that teach about the *Mayflower*, the Pilgrims, Native Americans, and the first Thanksgiving. Your students will pretend to sail across the sea on the *Mayflower*, explore Pilgrim and Native American homes, make an authentic Pilgrim recipe, and find out fascinating facts—and folklore—about the Pilgrims and the first Thanksgiving. Children also make a collaborative class banner that lets them personally reflect on the meaning of this holiday and a mini-book that invites them to interview family members to learn how Thanksgiving traditions form and change. Other fun features that will enrich your curriculum include:

♦ A big, colorful pocket chart poetry poster that lets kids count down to Thanksgiving

♦ Easy and festive art projects that kids can take home

♦ Engaging math and science activities

♦ Lively literature links

♦ Intriguing Internet resources

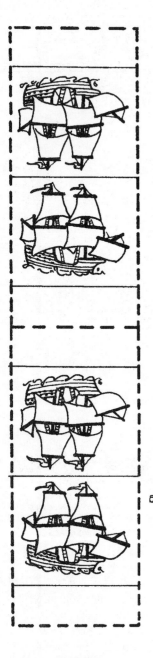

Journey to a New World

"Sail on the *Mayflower*!" Game
(Social Studies and Math)

Let children learn about the Pilgrims' voyage on the *Mayflower* with this easy-to-play game. Reproduce pages 16 and 17. Line up the pages as indicated, and tape them together. Glue onto lightweight cardboard, or laminate for added durability. (Make multiple game boards so that several groups can play at once, if desired.) Use a brass fastener and a paper clip to put together the spinner as shown. Photocopy and cut out the *Mayflower* markers along the dotted lines (left). Fold and tape to make them stand up.

Give a game board to each group of two or three children. Players put their ships on START. The first player spins and moves the number of spaces shown on the spinner, then follows any instructions on the space he or she lands on. As children play, they will learn about the experiences of the Pilgrims as they made their voyage to America. The game is over when all players have made it to America.

What Did the Pilgrims Pack?
(Social Studies)

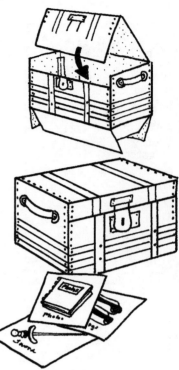

Historians estimate that the *Mayflower* was only about 90 feet long and 25 feet wide and carried 102 passengers and 20-plus crew members. Because space on the ship was limited, the Pilgrims could only pack a few important items to bring with them to America. Invite children to pretend they are Pilgrims with a trunk to pack for their voyage. Enlarge and copy page 18 for each child. Have children glue the trunk pattern onto half of a file folder and cut it out. Model how to assemble the trunk as shown. Then give children each a copy of page 19. Ask them to cut out items they think the Pilgrims might have brought with them to America and pack them in their trunks. Invite children to draw pictures of other items to add as well. Afterward, ask children to explain their choices. (Possible choices include: water, dried meat and fish, cheese and dried biscuits, cradle, axe, sword, knife, clothing, iron pot.)

Parchment Paper Classroom Compact
(Social Studies and Art)

Before the Pilgrims got off the ship, their leaders wrote the Mayflower Compact, a document that was signed by all of the passengers. In it they agreed that laws would be made for the good of the colony and that everyone would obey them. Ask children why they think it was important for the Pilgrims to have such rules to follow. Why is it important to have classroom rules? Then, together, draw up a Classroom Compact. On the chalkboard, list rules children think are important for their class to follow. Record your compact on authentic-looking old paper (see directions, right). When the compact is complete, invite each child to sign it. Hang it in a prominent place in your classroom.

Parchment Paper

Tear open a brown grocery bag to make a flat sheet of paper. Crumple the paper into a ball. Mix about two spoonfuls of soil into a bowl of warm water. Dip the paper in the water and then spread it out to dry on a plastic garbage bag.

Paper Windows for the Pilgrims
(Social Studies and Science)

The Pilgrims built simple wooden houses that had thatched roofs, made of coarse grass or cattails, and small windows. They used oiled paper for windowpanes because they had no glass. Let students make their own Pilgrim houses to find out how oil helps filter light.

1. Give each student a copy of page 20 and crayons. Tell children to outline the windows of their house with crayon.

Let children create colorful stained-glass turkeys using the turkey pattern on page 32. (Mask the writing lines before photocopying.) Have students color their turkey however they wish with crayons (pressing firmly). Then rub oil over each child's paper. Let dry, and display in a window.

2. Provide scissors, glue, and a 2- by 3-inch piece of light-colored construction paper.

3. Have children cut the flap door along the dotted lines and fold it back along the solid line. Model how to glue the construction paper onto the back of the house so it covers the opening. Trim off the excess.

4. Let children draw Pilgrims inside the house and then close the door. Children may also glue dried grass or raffia to the roof, if desired.

5. Cover a table with newspaper. Dab a cotton ball dipped in vegetable oil gently over the windows on each child's house.

6. Let the windowpanes dry a bit, and then tape the Pilgrim houses to the windows of your classroom. Ask: "What did the oil do to the paper?" (*It soaked into it and allowed some light to pass through.*) To see the Pilgrim families, invite children to open the doors of the houses.

The Pilgrims made wood houses. The roofs were made of grass. They used oiled paper as windows because they had no glass.

Wetu Means "House"
(Social Studies)

When the Pilgrims settled in America, they were helped by the Wampanoag (WAHM-puh-NOH-ahg) Indians. The Wampanoag "People of the Dawn") lived in a dwelling called a *wetu*, their word for *house*. To build a wetu, they bent wood poles cut from trees and stuck them in the ground to make a dome shape. Then they covered this framework with mats made of woven plants or tree bark. Mats were also hung in the doorways to keep out wind. A wetu was often as big as 13 feet wide and 16 feet long. As many as 10 people lived inside.

Let children make their own wetu. Have children follow steps 2 and 3 in the Paper Windows for the Pilgrims activity (see above), using the wetu pattern on page 21. Let them color the wetu brown, draw Wampanoag Indians inside the house, and glue on pieces of dried grass or raffia, if desired.

Discuss the wetu's dome shape. If possible, show children other dome-shaped structures such as the United States Capitol and various sports arenas. Then have children compare and contrast the wetu with the Pilgrim house.

The Wampanoag lived in a wetu. It was where they made their home. They bent poles cut from trees To make its shape a dome.

Foods for a Feast

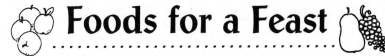

"Giving Thanks Around the Year" Write-and-Read Book

(Language Arts and Social Studies)

"We have lived with this land for thousands of generations, fishing in the waters, planting and harvesting crops, hunting the four-legged and winged beings, and giving respect and thanks for each and every thing taken for our use."

—Nanepashemet, Wampanoag historian

The Wampanoag celebrated many "Thanksgivings" long before the arrival of the Pilgrims in 1620. At these seasonal harvest festivals, still celebrated throughout the year, the Wampanoag express their gratitude for the gifts of the land. For example, in July they celebrate a Green Corn Thanksgiving (green corn is immature, but edible and sweet). In October they have a Cranberry Thanksgiving. Explain to children that the Wampanoag harvest and hunt different foods in each season.

Have children make their books. (See How to Make the Books, right.) Read pages 1, 3, 5, and 7 together. On each of these pages, children can draw pictures representing the seasonal foods listed. Then, on pages 2, 4, 6, and 8, children can write and illustrate things they are thankful for during each season. Encourage them to think of gifts from nature, such a warm, summer sun or a delicious food that comes from the earth. When children are finished, invite them to share their books with classmates and then add them to your class library.

Harvest Sort

(Math)

Use traditional Thanksgiving foods to let children practice classification skills. Have children work in small groups. Give each group an empty egg carton and a plastic sandwich bag filled with a variety of harvest foods, such as assorted nuts, cranberries, Indian corn kernels (or colored popcorn kernels), puffed popcorn, and pumpkin seeds. How many different ways can children find to sort the foods into the egg carton cups? Ask children to record their ideas as they work (color, shape, size, kind of food, and so on). Afterward, let each group share the ways they grouped the foods. After completing this activity, children can use these materials to make Patterned Place Cards (see page 10).

How to Make the Books

Give each student a two-sided photocopy of pages 23–26. (You'll need to remove the Write-and-Read Book pages from the book.) Also provide each student with an 8½- by 11-inch sheet of construction paper and crayons or colored pencils. To make a cover, have students fold the construction paper in half the short way and write the title "Giving Thanks Around the Year." Then model how to assemble the books. Fold pages 1 to 4 and 5 to 8 in half along the dotted lines, keeping the folds to the left side. Place pages 1 to 4 in front of pages 5 to 8. Place the book pages inside the front and back covers. Check to be sure that the pages are in the proper order, and then staple them together along the book's spine.

Thanksgiving Vegetable Platter
(Science)

At the first Thanksgiving, the Pilgrims celebrated their bountiful first harvest of fruits and vegetables. Some vegetables, such as potatoes, are the roots of a plant. Others come from a plant's leaf, stem, root, fruit, or flower. Write the words for plant parts across the top of a chart, leaving room in the left-hand column for plant names. Ask children to name different vegetables and fruits. Then help them decide which part of a plant each food comes from.

PLANT	leaf	stem	root	seed	fruit	flower
spinach	✓					
pumpkin					✓	
corn				✓		
celery		✓				

Plant Parts

Leaves:
lettuce, cabbage, spinach

Stems:
celery, asparagus,
sugar (from cane)

Roots:
radish, potato, onion,
carrot, beet

Seeds:
flour, peanuts, corn,
peas, beans, bran

Fruits:
pumpkin, peach, cherry,
apple, banana

Flowers:
broccoli, cauliflower

Safety Note

Check for possible allergies before doing activities that involve children tasting different foods.

No-Cook Recipe: Harvest Trail Mix
(Social Studies)

Nuts, pumpkins, cranberries, currants, and corn were among the foods consumed by the Pilgrims and Wampanoag. When the growing season was over, the fruits were often dried and preserved for later use. Invite students to taste these foods. Set out bowls of dried cranberries, currants or raisins, popcorn, nuts, and pumpkin seeds, with a plastic spoon in each. Let children put a spoonful of each item into a small paper cup. (For added fun, serve the snacks in Pilgrim Hat Snack Holders, page 12.)

A Pilgrim Recipe: Red Pickled Eggs
(Cooking and Science)

The Pilgrims loved spicy food. They brought with them on the *Mayflower* spices such as pepper, cloves, cinnamon, nutmeg, and ginger. Spices made their food more flavorful and were useful in masking the flavor of foods that had begun to rot. Invite children to try an authentic Pilgrim delicacy, red pickled eggs! Give each child a copy of the recipe on page 22. Prepare the eggs in class, or suggest that children prepare this 400-year-old recipe with an adult family member at home to serve at their holiday meal. As they make this dish, encourage children to observe how the ingredients change in the process (beets turn vinegar mixture reddish purple, eggs change color, and so on). This recipe was adapted from *Eating the Plates: A Pilgrim Book of Food and Manners* by Lucille Recht Penner (Macmillan, 1991), a fascinating book that offers a wealth of information about the food preparation, cooking techniques, and home life of the Pilgrims.

◆ Close-Up on Cranberries ◆

TIP

Make pop-up pumpkin books using an orange pumpkin-shaped template.

Pop-Up Cranberry Books
(Language Arts)

Invite children to make cranberry pop-up books to write in as they explore this traditional Thanksgiving fruit. Use coffee can lids as templates. Have children trace four circles on red construction paper, cut them out, stack them, and fold them in half. Open the pages and staple along the fold. Make the books stand up by spreading the pages apart.

Do the Cranberry Bounce!
(Math)

To harvest cranberries, farmers flood cranberry bogs with water. The berries float, making them easy to corral with large tools called booms. To check the berries for quality, cranberry processors bounce them! Each berry has seven chances to bounce over four-inch "bounce boards." A badly bruised or rotten berry will not bounce. Students can test whether cranberries bounce by dropping them from a height of 12 inches next to a ruler and then measuring how high the berries bounce. Invite children to speculate about why the berries bounce. Then cut several berries in half for students to examine. Point out the hard cell walls around the air pockets inside. Explain that when these walls start to break down and soften, the berries will no longer bounce.

Cranberry Count-Up
(Math)

Divide the class into small groups and give each a one-pound bag of fresh cranberries. Let students pass around the bag and estimate the number of cranberries it holds. Have them record their estimates. Then ask students how they might find the actual number (count the berries one by one, count by 2s, 5s, 10s; fill a container, such as a 1/4-cup measure, with berries, count the number of berries it holds, then find out how many 1/4-cup measures fill the bag, and so on). Let each group choose a method to use. Afterward, have each group compare its estimates with the results. Ask each group to describe the advantages and disadvantages of the method used. Also compare the number of berries in each bag. Can students account for the differences given that each bag weighs one pound?

Craft Corner

Patterned Place Cards
(Art and Math)

Invite children to practice patterning while making festive place cards for their family's holiday table. Set out bowls of harvest foods. (Use the items left over from the Harvest Sort activity, page 7.) Give children each a paper cup to collect items they want to work with, and a paper plate. Have them experiment with making different patterns on their plate. Then provide 4- by 6-inch unlined index cards, glue, and crayons or markers. Have children fold the cards in half. Tell them to use the items to make a patterned border around one side of the card. Once they have decided on a pattern they would like to keep, have children glue the items onto their cards.

Plant-Pigment Napkin Rings
(Art and Social Studies)

TIP

Check florists' shops, garden centers, and grocery stores for flowers, vegetables, fruits, and other plants that would otherwise be thrown away. Send home a note requesting donations. Plant parts that work well include geranium petals, grass cuttings, spinach leaves, cranberries, tea leaves, coffee grounds, parsley, onion skins, red cabbage leaves, and beets.

It's a popular notion that Pilgrims wore only dark, somber colors such as brown and black. In fact, red, blue, yellow, violet, and green are also among the colors they wore. The Pilgrims used flowers, leaves, roots, bark, nutshells, and berries to dye the yarn or fabric they made into clothing. Invite children to explore the natural pigments in plants as they make festive holiday napkin rings.

Materials
assorted plant parts (See Tip, left)
plastic sandwich bags
muslin or old white cotton pillowcases or sheets cut into 2¼- by 6-inch
   strips (use pinking shears or scalloped scissors for an interesting effect)
cardboard bathroom tissue tubes, cut in half crosswise
glue
cotton swabs (optional)
paper and pencil

1. Place a few pieces of one kind of plant in each plastic bag. Label each bag with the plant's name.
2. Divide the class into groups. Give each group a few bags of plant samples. Ask children how they might find out what colors, if any, these plants produce (squeeze between fingers, rub on paper).

3. Ask children to predict what color each plant might make. Will all the red plant parts produce red pigments? How about the green plants? After recording plant names and predictions, students can test the plant parts by rubbing them on their papers.

4. Bring students together to share their discoveries. What plants produced surprising colors?

5. Give students fabric strips and plant pigments to make napkin rings. Cotton swabs are useful for rubbing plant pigments into the cloth. When the fabric strips are dry, let children glue them onto bathroom tissue tubes.

Good-Deed Bead Necklaces
(Social Studies and Art)

The Wampanoag Indians used wampum—white and purple beads made from quahog (clam) shells—as symbols of power and authority. Wampum was later used as money. In the spirit of Thanksgiving, children can reward each other with a wampum bead each time they see a classmate perform a good deed. Good deeds might include sharing materials, helping a classmate clean up, and so on. To make purple wampum, fill a shallow pan halfway with water. Mix in several drops each of blue and red food coloring. Dip pasta (*ditalini* or *penne* work well) and let dry on paper towels. Help children cut lengths of yarn to tie loosely around the neck. Each time a child does a good deed, he or she can add a bead to the necklace!

Perky Turkey Puppet
(Art and Poetry)

Children will giggle and "gobble" as they play with these delightful puppets. Enlarge and photocopy page 27 onto heavyweight paper (one per student). Or have each child glue the page onto half of a file folder and wait until dry. Let children color the patterns and then cut them out. (Children may need help cutting out the slots. Gently fold the paper at a right angle to the dotted lines. Then snip along the lines from the crease of the fold inward.) Model for children how to put the turkey together, following these diagrams. To make the turkey move its neck and flap its tail, pull on its feet.

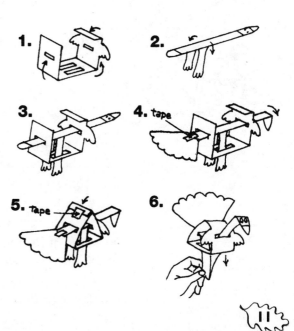

Pilgrim Hat Snack Holders
(Art)

Children will love making these simple snack holders to use in class or to bring home! Cut an empty bathroom tissue tube in half crosswise. Paint the outside black and let dry. Cut a 3½-inch circle of black construction paper for the brim. Center the tube on the circle and glue or tape the crown in place. Add a white paper band. Fill with Harvest Trail Mix. (See page 8.)

"Fact or Folklore?" Turkey Teller
(Social Studies and Art)

Invite children and their families to find out little-known facts—and folklore—about the Pilgrims and the first Thanksgiving. Let children make these turkey tellers to bring home and share on Thanksgiving Day. Enlarge and photocopy page 28 for each child. Have children cut out the pattern along the dotted lines. Tell them to place the pattern blank side up on a flat surface. Then model how to make the turkey tellers, following these diagrams:

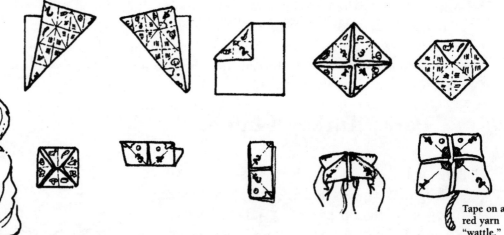

Tape on a red yarn "wattle."

How to Play
Hold the turkey teller as shown. Have someone (the player) choose one of the numbers. Open and close the turkey teller that number of times. Then have the player look inside and choose a picture. Open and close the turkey teller the number of letters that spell the name of that picture (for example, if the picture is a fish, open and close it four times—F-I-S-H). Repeat the process. Then the player chooses another picture. Open the panel and read what's underneath. The player must say whether the statement is fact (true) or folklore (not true).

Perfect Poetry

Pocket Chart Poetry Poster: "I Can Hardly Wait!"
(Language Arts)

Count down to Thanksgiving with your class by sharing this playful rhyme that's just right for emergent readers. Follow these steps to set up pocket chart activities with the poem (bound in the center of the book):

1. Laminate the poster or glue it onto a piece of lightweight cardboard. Cut apart the sentence strips and cards. Arrange the sentence strips in order in a pocket chart. Place the word, numeral, and picture cards at the bottom of the chart. Display a calendar opened to November.

2. A few days before Thanksgiving, look at the calendar with children. Together, count the number of days until Thanksgiving. Then ask children to name foods their families might eat on Thanksgiving Day.

3. Read aloud the poem to children. Invite a volunteer to select the appropriate word or numeral card to complete the first blank. If the child chooses the numeral card (3), ask the class if there is another card that shows the same number (three).

4. Continue reading, then let another child choose a word or picture card to complete the third line.

5. As a class, read the completed poem aloud. Then let children take turns choosing a favorite word or picture card to complete the third line.

6. Repeat the activity daily, up to the day before Thanksgiving. (On that day, use a self-sticking note to mask the *s* in the word *days*.)

Variations

- After everyone has had a turn, place the pocket chart in a center and invite children to work with partners to put the poem together.

- Start the activity more than seven days before Thanksgiving. Make additional word and and numeral cards using index cards trimmed to size.

- Invite children to create different word or picture cards for other favorite Thanksgiving foods.

- Extend the activity by having children sort the foods into different groups (meats, vegetables, breads, and so on).

- Mix up a completed version of the poem so that the sentence strips are out of order. Let children come up to the chart and reorder the poem line by line.

✿ I Can Hardly Wait! ✿					
_____ more days till Thanksgiving.					
I can hardly wait!					
I will have some _____.					
It will be so great!					
Seven	Six	Five	Four	Three	Two
7	6	5	4	3	2
One	I	pie		peas	
stuffing		cranberries			
apple cider		mashed potatoes			
turkey		corn bread			

EXPLORE MORE!

Use children's choices to make a Favorite Thanksgiving Foods graph. Remove the sentence strips and place the pictures side by side at the bottom of the pocket chart. Have children write their names on self-sticking notes. Then invite them to come up to the chart one by one and place their name above their favorite food. Next, invite children to analyze the data on the graph. Ask questions, such as:

- How many children like [stuffing] best?

- Which Thanksgiving food do most children like best? Least?

- How many more/fewer children prefer [turkey] than prefer [corn bread]?

Song: "Thanksgiving Day"
(Music and Poetry)

Children will love singing this song to the familiar tune of "Here We Go 'Round the Mulberry Bush." To perform the song, divide the class into five groups. Have the students in the first group join hands as they sing their verse. The second group then joins hands with the first group, and so on. When the last verse is sung, have everyone join hands to form a circle. Afterward, give children a chance to reflect on what they are thankful for by making a "We Give Thanks" collaborative banner (see below).

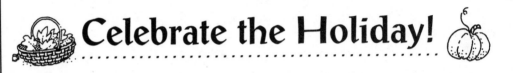

Celebrate the Holiday!

"We Give Thanks" Collaborative Banner
(Writing)

This Thanksgiving banner is a delightful invitation to children to reflect on the holiday, read, write, and share! Make a copy of page 30 for each child. Read the prompt on the pattern page with your class. Let children use developmental spelling to write their responses on scrap paper. Children who are not yet writing can dictate their responses to you. Help children edit their work, copy the edited version onto the pattern page, and illustrate it with crayons, markers, or colored pencils. Let children help put the banner together by taping their pattern pages to the others. Display the banner on a bulletin board or wall, from the ceiling, or in the hallway.

Or, instead of taping, simply clip the pages side by side on a clothesline strung across your classroom in an area that's away from traffic.

Before children go home for the holiday, give them their completed page along with extra blank copies for family

EXPLORE MORE!

- Ask children to point out the rhyming words in the song. List each rhyming group on a separate sheet of chart paper. Then ask students to identify ways in which the words in each group are alike and different. For example, *those, goes,* and *clothes* all contain the long-*o* sound, but each word has a different spelling pattern. Use the lists to start rhyming word walls. Invite children to add to each list as they discover new rhyming words. (Students may also want to create personal mini word walls using the Turkey Stationery on page 32.)

- Point out the digraph *th* in *Thanksgiving*. Explain that this consonant pair stands for one sound. A digraph can appear at the beginning, in the middle, or at the end of a word. Ask children to find other words in the song that begin with this digraph. (*thanks, the, this, those, clothes,* and *with*)

14

members. Suggest that children invite each of their family members to complete a pattern. The pages can then be used as festive and meaningful place mats for their holiday celebrations. (Suggest that children glue the completed patterns onto sheets of construction paper.)

Thanksgiving Memories Mini-Book

(Language Arts and Writing)

Students develop a sense of history by learning about holiday traditions celebrated today and in the past. Invite students to interview an older family member, such as a grandparent, or an older family friend about his or her Thanksgiving memories. Let children make and take home the mini-book on page 31. Consider making multiple copies so that children may interview several people. To make the book, cut out the pattern along the dotted lines. Fold along the solid lines so that the pages go from 1 to 4.

Turkey Stationery

(Writing)

The turkey stationery on page 32 can be used in myriad ways to build literacy. Stock a writing-paper bin with copies that students can use to write letters, stories, poems, journal entries, and class newsletters. Students can also use the sheets to create word lists, greeting cards, invitations, classroom displays, banners, and more.

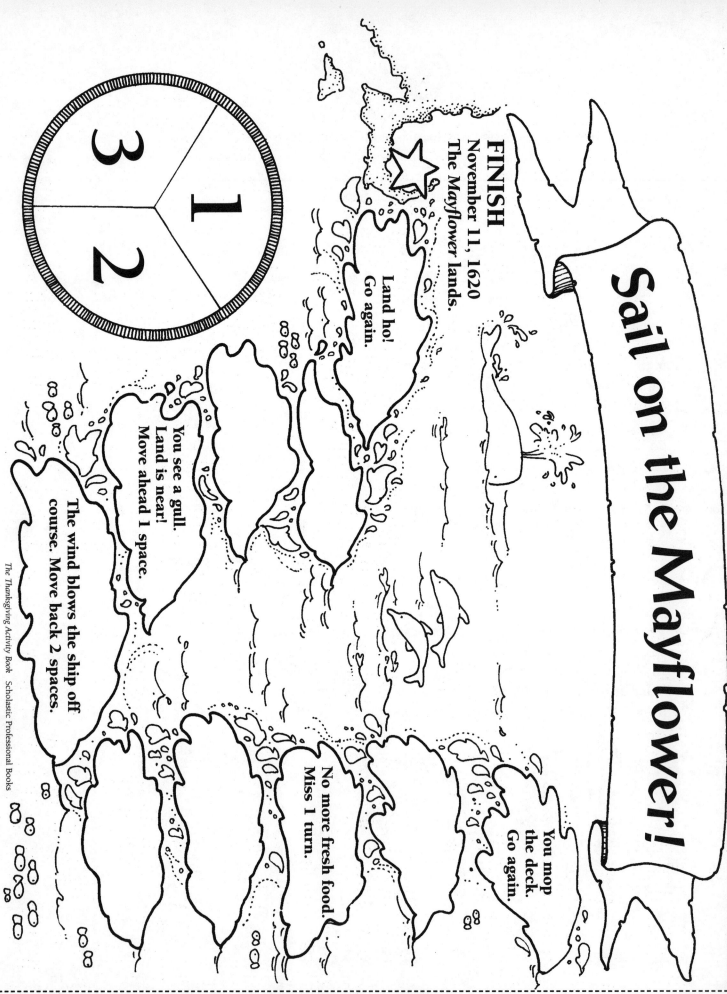

Sail on the Mayflower!

FINISH
November 11, 1620
The Mayflower lands.

Land ho!
Go again.

You see a gull.
Land is near!
Move ahead 1 space.

The wind blows the ship off
course. Move back 2 spaces.

No more fresh food.
Miss 1 turn.

You mop
the deck.
Go again.

1
3
2

The Thanksgiving Activity Book Scholastic Professional Books

Align top of page 17 here and tape in place.

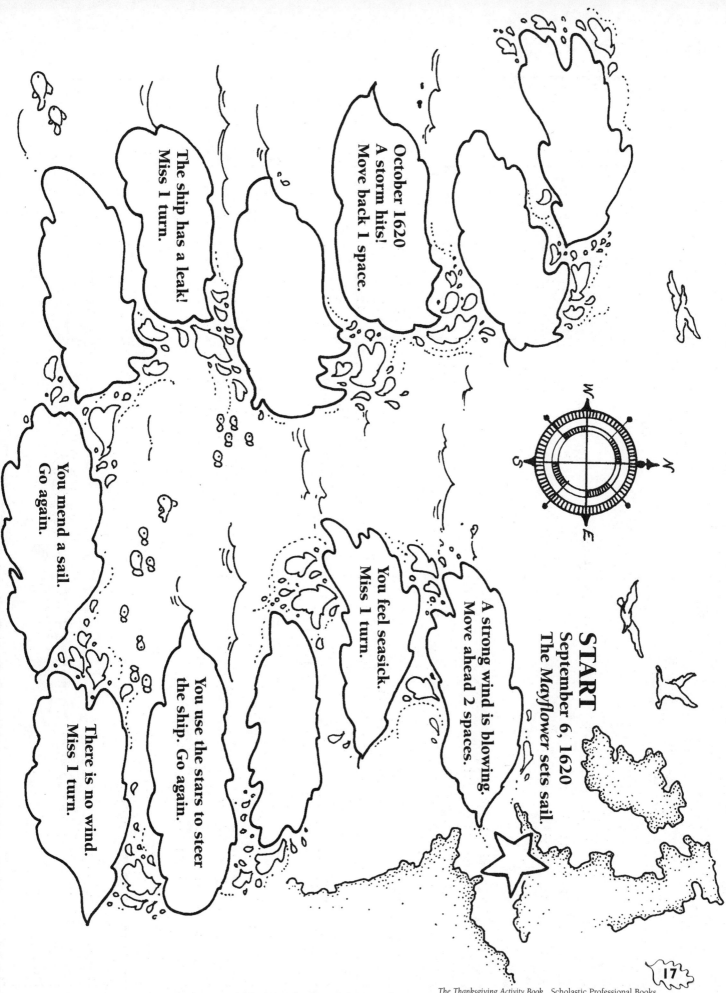

The ship has a leak!
Miss 1 turn.

October 1620
A storm hits!
Move back 1 space.

You mend a sail.
Go again.

You feel seasick.
Miss 1 turn.

There is no wind.
Miss 1 turn.

You use the stars to steer
the ship. Go again.

A strong wind is blowing.
Move ahead 2 spaces.

START
September 6, 1620
The *Mayflower* sets sail.

The Thanksgiving Activity Book Scholastic Professional Books

Pilgrim Trunk Pattern

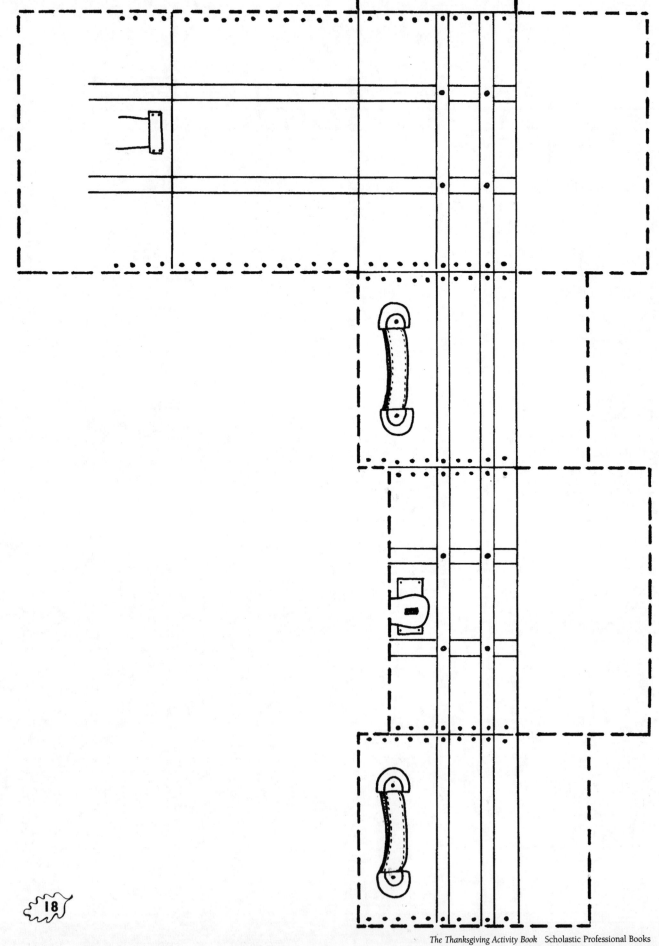

Name_____

What Did the Pilgrims Pack?

What did the Pilgrims take with them to America?
Cut out the pictures and put them in your trunk.

Water	Hot dogs and buns	Cradle
Computer	Clothing	Knife
Sword	Dried meat and fish, cheese, dried biscuits	Photo album
Phone	Iron pot	Axe

Pilgrim House Pattern

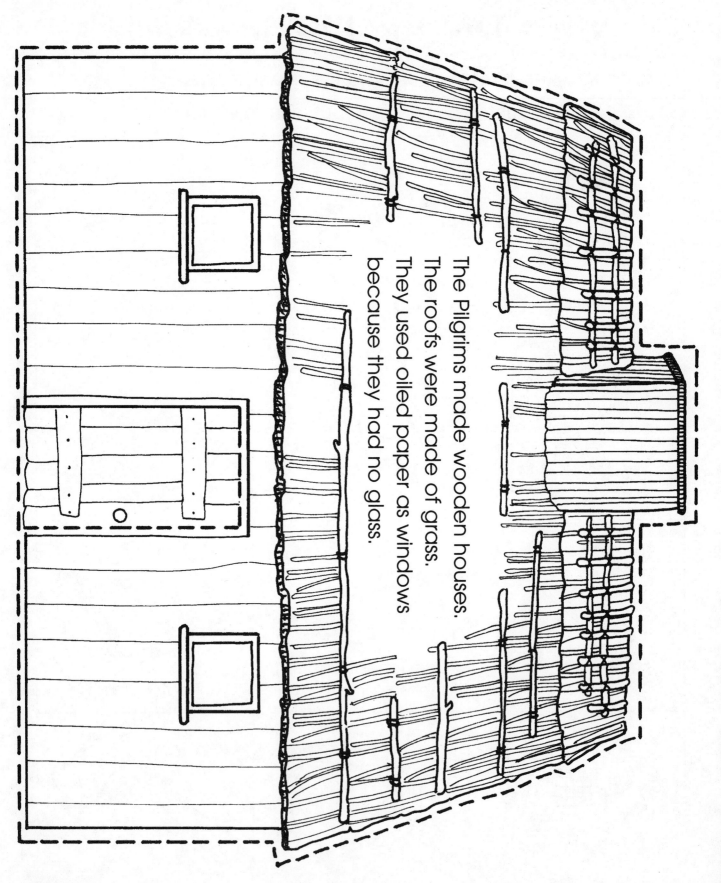

The Pilgrims made wooden houses.
The roofs were made of grass.
They used oiled paper as windows
because they had no glass.

Wetu Pattern

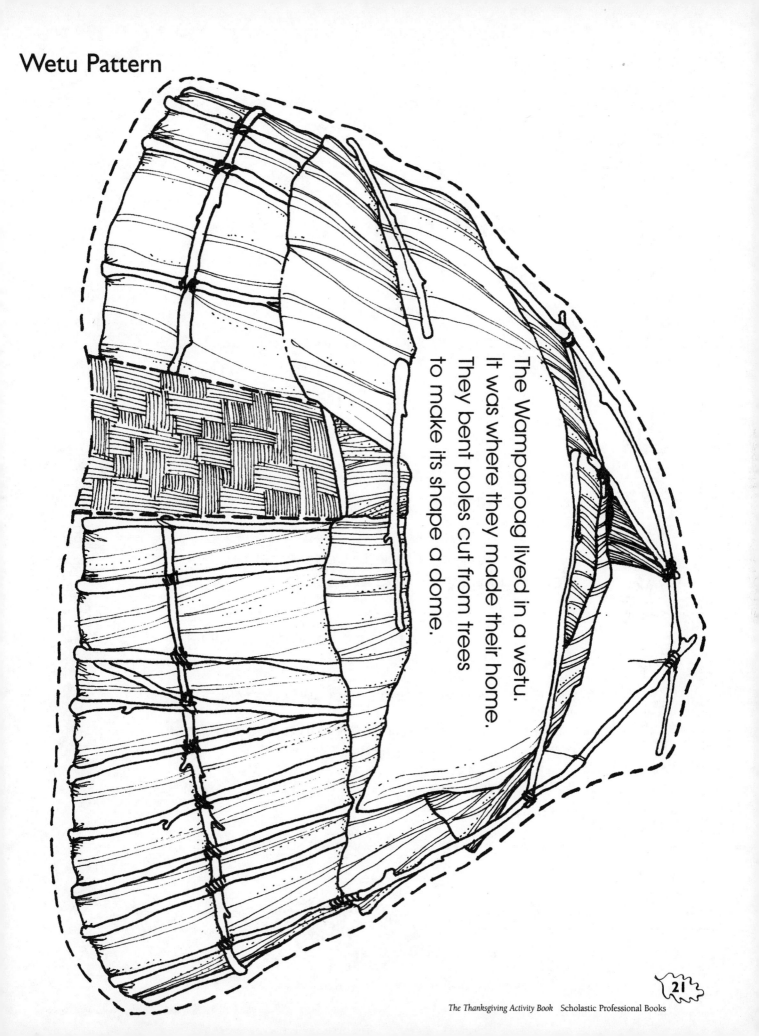

The Wampanoag lived in a wetu.
It was where they made their home.
They bent poles cut from trees
to make its shape a dome.

A Pilgrim Recipe:
Red Pickled Eggs
~ Serves 6 ~

What You Need:

6 peeled, hard-boiled eggs

1 small beet

1 cup white vinegar

1 teaspoon salt

$\frac{1}{2}$ teaspoon black pepper

$\frac{1}{2}$ teaspoon red pepper

1 cup water

1. Wash dirt off the beet with a soft vegetable brush. Cut off the top. Then cut the stem so that only one inch of stem remains.

2. Mix the vinegar, salt, black and red pepper, and one cup water in a saucepan. Bring to a boil. Then turn off the heat.

3. Put the eggs and the beet into a heat-resistant glass jar or container with a lid. Pour the hot vinegar mixture over them.

Safety Note: The mixture and the jar will be very hot!

4. Let the jar cool down. Stir gently with a wooden spoon. Cover the jar and refrigerate overnight.

5. In the morning, remove the beet from the jar. How have the eggs changed?

6. Slice the eggs in half and serve with salad.

Recipe adapted from *Eating the Plates: A Pilgrim Book of Manners* by Lucille Recht Penner (Macmillan, 1991)

In winter, the Wampanoag give thanks for deer, turkeys, eels, and clams.

1

In spring, I give thanks for

_____

_____

_____

4

2

In winter, I give thanks for

_____

_____

_____

3

In spring, the Wampanoag give thanks for herring, a kind of fish, and new plants that grow.

In fall, the Wampanoag give thanks for squash, corn, string beans, nuts, and cranberries.

7

In summer, I give thanks for

_____

_____

_____

6

In fall, I give thanks for

8

In summer, the Wampanoag
give thanks for berries and
green corn.

5

Perky Turkey Puppet

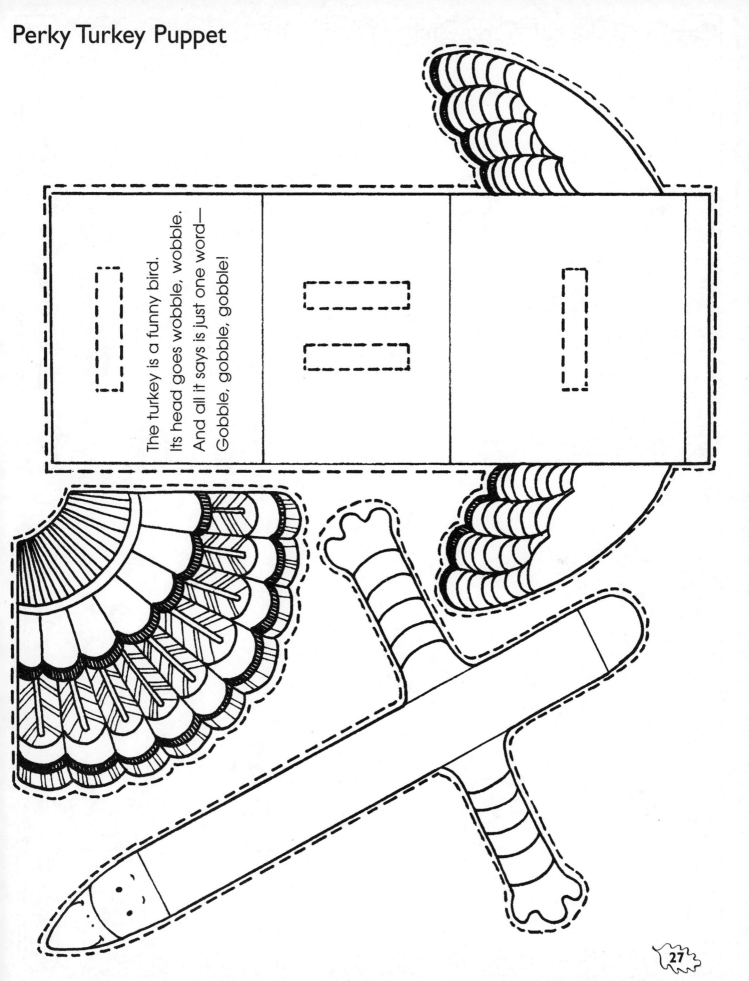

The turkey is a funny bird.
Its head goes wobble, wobble.
And all it says is just one word—
Gobble, gobble, gobble!

The Thanksgiving Activity Book Scholastic Professional Books

"Fact or Folklore?" Turkey Teller

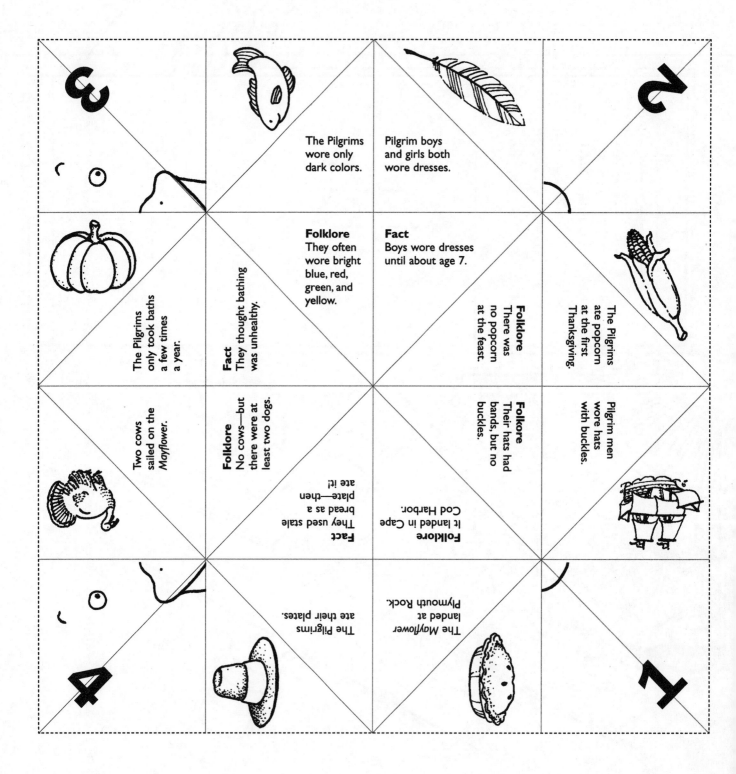

3

The Pilgrims wore only dark colors.

Pilgrim boys and girls both wore dresses.

2

Folklore They often wore bright blue, red, green, and yellow.

Fact Boys wore dresses until about age 7.

Folklore There was no popcorn at the feast.

The Pilgrims ate popcorn at the first Thanksgiving.

The Pilgrims only took baths a few times a year.

Fact They thought bathing was unhealthy.

Two cows sailed on the *Mayflower*.

Folklore No cows—but there were at least two dogs.

Fact They used stale bread as a plate—then ate it!

Folklore It landed in Cape Cod Harbor.

Folklore Their hats had bands, but no buckles.

Pilgrim men wore hats with buckles.

4

The Pilgrims ate their plates.

The *Mayflower* landed at Plymouth Rock.

1

The Thanksgiving Activity Book Scholastic Professional Books

Thanksgiving Day

(Sing to the tune of "Here We Go 'Round the Mulberry Bush")

This is the day for giving thanks,
Giving thanks, giving thanks.
This is the day for giving thanks,
We celebrate Thanksgiving!

This is the day for thanking those
Who give us food and give us clothes.
This is the day a "thank you" goes
To family on Thanksgiving!

This is the day for thanking friends,
On friendship, everyone depends.
This is the day our thanks extend
To friends on Thanksgiving!

This is the day the Pilgrims ate,
And with the Wampanoag shared their plate.
This is the day we commemorate
The very first Thanksgiving!

This is the day to be sincere,
Give thanks that we are here.
In November every year
We celebrate Thanksgiving!

—Meish Goldish

We Give Thanks

For family and friends,
pie and turkey, too.
Thanksgiving's the time
we say thank you!

I am thankful for

_____

Name

Thanksgiving Memories Mini-Book Pattern

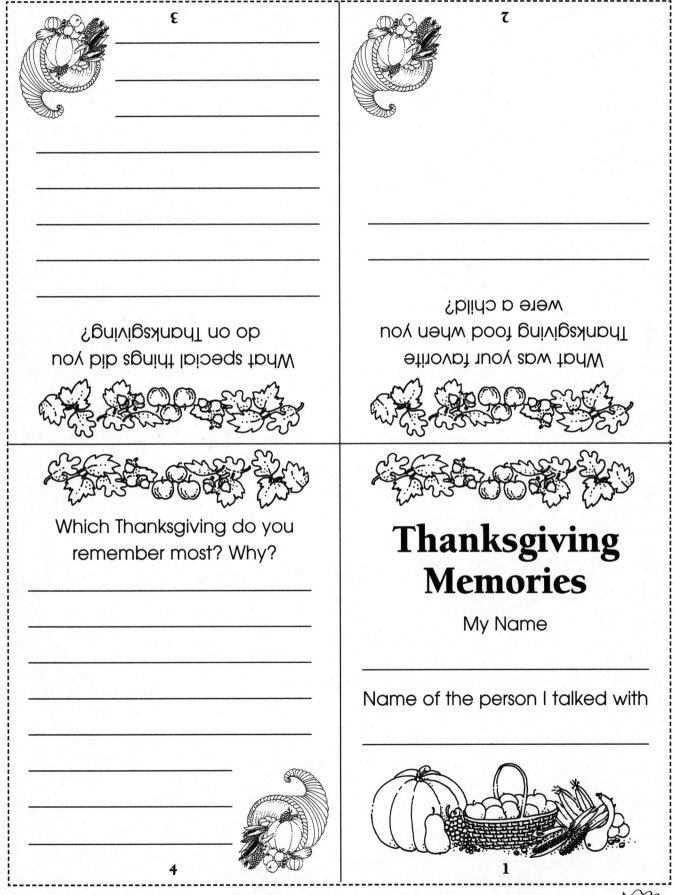

3

_____

_____

_____

_____

_____

What special things did you
do on Thanksgiving?

2

_____

_____

What was your favorite
Thanksgiving food when you
were a child?

Which Thanksgiving do you
remember most? Why?

_____

_____

_____

_____

_____

_____

4

Thanksgiving
Memories

My Name

_____

Name of the person I talked with

_____

1

Turkey Stationery